Let's Kick Anxiety's Butt.

An interactive way to overcome
anxiety and feel truly happy.

SAMANTHA HEARNE

ISBN: 978-1-9164283-0-0

First published 2018

CONTENTS

I wasn't sure whether to include this or not, but the more I thought about it, the more I had to.

I just want to set the scene for you, because I want nothing more than to empower you to know that ANYTHING IS POSSIBLE, when your mind-set is working for you, not against you.

I have gone back to add this page after I completed a line reading 'nothing changes, if you change nothing.'

I couldn't stop thinking about this and how it changed my life. Genuinely changed my life.

I spent over 10 years worrying about pleasing other people, letting people down, not being good enough for someone, being judged, not being accepted, fear of being abandoned, doubting myself, not being able to be alone – honestly the list goes on and on, but the bottom line is, I have 100% been where you are now my lovely. Like 100, million%.

Life handed me some very raw deals, dealt me cards that I wish I could have ripped up, situations I didn't even think I could handle at 50, let alone 15!

Throughout it all, something stuck with me, my true sense of self. Who I wanted to be. What I wanted to become in life. How I wanted my future to be.

Although anxiety, fear, grief, insecurity stopped me from pursuing these things, they still lingered. Until one day I realised that I had to change something. I had to do the hard work and stop waiting, stop wishing, stop hoping. I took action.

If you are holding this book in your hand, or reading this book on your device, know that THIS is your first step, YOUR action.

I have created a successful coaching business, thriving Podcast channel and spoken at huge events across the UK, as well as write for 5 mental health magazines, all whilst working full time as a secondary school teacher, with a huge responsibility attached to that too!

I have written the first 70 pages of the book, at my office desk, before school at 6.30am, in my lunchbreak and in-between clients and live video sessions over weekends. I chose. I chose change. I chose impact.

If you truly want something to change, you can make it. If you really want bigger and better things for yourself and your future – you can make that happen. Trust me.

I am living proof of that and I will do everything in my power to give you back your self-belief within this book.

Anxiety stripped away so much from me, and I don't want that for you. I am here to give you the solutions I spent years trying to find and support you.

Every. Single. Step. Of. The. Way.
That is my promise to you.

Getting Stuck In

Part 1

SELFIE CHALLENGE

Right – before we dive into this book and change your life, I HAVE to know who you are, what you look like and become your BFF! I am being deadly serious!

So... challenge 1.

(If you are serious about overcoming anxiety, get ready for lots of challenges and being held to account!)

You need to take a selfie with this book, (you can be as creative, fun and whacky as you like – in fact, I encourage that) and post it onto my Facebook Biz Page (www.facebook.com/AHappyMind1) and tag me on Instagram (www.instagram.com/a.happy.mind) because, let's face it, by the end of this book you will know A LOT about me and my journey and I want to know who I am talking to!

GO!

YOUR TOOLKIT

Have you ever read a self-development book, taken lots of notes, highlighted the pages, taken photos of key parts and then... nothing! I know I have.

I will take snippets of each book and remember the bits that stood out most to me for as long as I possibly can, but actually creating new and lasting habits was difficult.

So the next fundamental step is to make sure you are as prepared as possible for this book to change your life.

I want to set you up for success, not just an average result or outcome.

This is a toolkit you will need throughout this book and one that has served me very well over the past 5 years.

1. Big girl pants (if you are a man reading this, make sure your boxers are extra-large!)

You cannot go into this half-baked. You are committed or you are not. You must be willing to dig deep, be honest with yourself and with me and really do the work required to make lasting change. Your big girl pants will see you through the testing times and also reassure you, that this IS the best thing you could be doing for yourself. Honestly, the process can be hard work, but the harder you work, the more you will change your life. So go and grab your big girl pants and keep them on!

2. A trusted support

This process will be one that requires you to be open and honest with yourself, but for the most effective and lasting results, voicing what you learn and discover in this book with a trusted loved one, will reinforce that learning and also allow someone you love, to support you through this transformation. The externalising of your thoughts and progress is so important. It makes it real. It makes it happening. It makes it present in your life. THAT is the impact this process needs to have to change your life for good.

3. Commitment

You must dedicate time to read this book each and every day. Even if it is 2 pages a day. I need to be talking to you daily and having that continuity with you. Remember, we are changing your life for the better, that cannot happen one Saturday morning, or the odd Monday night. That needs to happen each and every day, so you show up just as much as I am and meet me here every single day. Your level of commitment to this book, will highlight just how much you are ready to change your life and take back control of your happiness.

4. Stationary

When you are reading this book, I want to be right there next to you. There will be tasks, questions and prompts for you to work through, throughout this book that are there for you to COMPLETE (not just skim past to get to the next page quicker!) I used to do this and it just stops you fully immersing yourself in the content and support I am here to give you. So take notes, highlight, underline, re-write into your own words – whatever will help you to cement and consolidate this journey for you.

5. Your 'Why'

When I first started to work on myself and combat anxiety, I had a really big reason why. My now husband. I wanted our relationship to be happy, healthy and full of fun not stress. Until I was willing to dig deep, work on myself and make the changes needed, our relationship continued to suffer. THIS was my big 'why'. I wanted a relationship that would last the test of time and thrive as we grew together, without anxiety being the third wheel.

My second 'why' was all about my future. I had spent 10 years constantly worrying about the past repeating itself, that it just stripped me of fully enjoying anything, in case it ended or went wrong. This was not how I wanted my life to be. My second 'why' was simply to be able to enjoy my life and be able to completely get lost in a moment or experience without the constant fear of something going wrong.

So tell me, what is your 'why' for reading this book?

Before you write anything, go and get;

Your big girl pants and put them on!

Share this 'why' with your trusted person and let them be there to encourage you to reach your 'why'.

Commit fully to this book, because your 'why' is your motivator.

Lastly – write it down with your stationary.

(See, you can already see the benefits of this toolkit and its only page 1!)

MY WHY

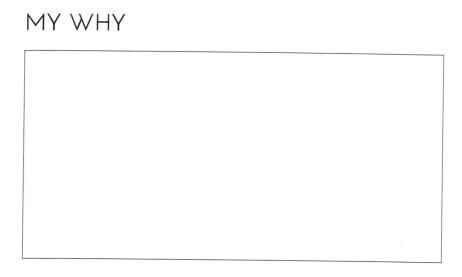

Character Profile (Sam Style!)

This book is like no other. It will be filled with my personality, my quirky ways and full blown honesty. I don't believe there is any other way to be with my community or clients, so I won't change for you either.

I am going to describe myself in 3 ways and at the end of these three profiles, I will be asking YOU a question. So pay close attention!

Sam No. 1

Sam is a risk taker, willing to make things happen for herself and not let other people or things stand in her way. She is determined to change her life, her mind-set and her relationships, and do whatever it takes to make that happen. Sam doesn't make excuses, doesn't listen to the 'what if' and goes and gets what she wants. Her future depends on these decisions, so Sam makes the decisions she knows will benefit her life most in the long run. No messing around.

Sam No. 2

Sam has lots of dreams. Lots of hopes and aspirations for herself. However, Sam just can't make them happen. Sam is a day dreamer and wishes for things to be better, but doesn't like change, so sticks to her everyday routine and lives in hope, not action. 'At least I know what I want and I know how I want to feel. At least I have a positive mind-set for my future and my goals.' These statements keep Sam from taking any risks or making things happen, and keeps her waiting for the change to happen for her, convinced that dreaming and wishing is enough.

Sam No 3

This Sam just has all the answers! I can't do that right now because I just don't have the time. Work is just too stressful for me right now, but in 6 months I'll be raring to go and make it happen. It sounds like a great idea in principle, but in reality surely it is more complicated, I just don't think I can waste time on something that isn't 100% proven, I'm just too busy. I know anxiety is part of who I am and I feel anxious a lot, but it's not just me, I'm not the only one, so it must just be how people are becoming these days. Let's just see how things go when work calms down, the kids are older, we have done our holidays, saved for a new extension and go from there.

Which Sam are you most like right now?

Which Sam do you think is going to change her life and create a happy and thriving future, anxiety free?

Which qualities do you need to embody whilst we go on this journey together?

I was in bed last night at 11pm (for some reason all my ideas spark up late at night) and I thought of three types of people and knew I had to share them with you in this book and really set the scene.

You have;

1. Go-Getters
2. Dream Creators
3. Excuse Makers

None of these profiles are bad people or negative, but now is the time to reflect and evaluate the type of profile you have been adopting and has it been working for you?

I am lucky enough to have always been a go-getter, no procrastination, just doing. This does mean my husband sometimes called me 'Slapdash Sam' because I can be impulsive and rush things, but at least I am starting. From a mistake, you can learn. From a quick decision, you can develop.

From an excuse – you gain nothing.

I didn't change my life by waiting. I had to work bloody hard to get to where I am now and if you want to watch a heartfelt, emotional and very raw video about my story and what lead me to where I am now – hop on over to my Facebook group and get to know me even more there. (www.facebook.com/AHappyMind1) To give you just a slice of what I mean by working bloody hard;

I worked 20 hours a week, whilst studying full time at university, as well as privately renting a flat in my final year and paying for myself to go to Australia for 3 weeks. I worked every summer holidays full time and saved the money for holidays with friends, to enjoy myself when I could.

I still graduated with a first class honours degree and set myself up as best I could for the adult world and getting my first teaching job.

1 month into my first teaching job I made myself homeless (I broke up with my long term boyfriend, who I lived with and his family and made the brave decision to take a risk and find my true soulmate.) This meant I then moved in with one of my dearest friends and her family. I spent Christmas with them for 5 years and I spent a year living there, whilst working at my first full time teaching job – far from an ideal way to start my career but I did it.

I still worked my summer and Easter holidays full time, whilst all other teachers were actually enjoying the holidays, I was working and managing a summer camp.

I was able to buy my first house at 23 and continued to work my socks off.

The point I am making, is this is not just about anxiety or mental health. This is about your life choices, the decisions you make daily, the hard work you put in, the investment you show to yourself and your future, your dedication for change, your drive for better and your passion for growth and progress.

I didn't settle in my career, my relationship, my future – why would I settle for emotions that don't make me happy or settle for a mind-set that makes me constantly doubt myself and feel like I am struggling.

'From an excuse -
you gain nothing'

So take some time to think about your life, the choices you have made and the lifestyle you have created for yourself.

Are you a;

1. Go-Getter
2. Dream Creator
3. Excuse Maker

How can you make small changes today, to show yourself that you matter most? Your happiness matters most. Your future is your priority.

It won't be easy but I promise you it will be worth it.

Some statements I used to face were;

'How can you afford to go to Australia at 21, you must have rich parents.'

Nope – I work full time and study full time, I just save my money.

'You are so lucky, you got on the property ladder so young.'

Nope – my Dad died when I was 14, my Mum sold our house when I was 20. The money I was left, I saved and didn't spend on partying, because I knew I had to look after myself.

'Wow, you have your own business and can leave teaching, I am so jealous.'

Jealous? I had to work 20 hour days, weekends, sacrifice time with my family and friends, invest time, effort and energy into making this a success. Are you doing those things too?

I could have easily lived a life of excuses, and been forgiven for doing so, but I didn't want my past to constantly dictate my present and my future. This was my life now, and I wanted to be in control of the outcome.

One more time – are you a;

1. Go-Getter
2. Dream Creator
3. Excuse Maker

QUICK FIRE TIPS

This book is here to be practical for you. I want to provide you with answers from the get-go (none of this, waiting until the end for the best bits!).

I do a lot of public speaking events and workshops and I always share my quick fire tips so that no person leaves me, the same way they came in. I want to impart knowledge and empower you to go forward and make change happen.

So these tips are purely here to give you a starting point. A base.

From each tip, we can dig deeper and make A LOT more progress, but at least you know you can start seeing results and shifting your mind-set in Part 1 of this fabulous (I know I'm biased) book!

1. Emotional Journal

Equipment needed;

- Your phone
- Your mind

I do this on my phone because it saves time and effort – and that's what you need right now!

I simply take notes on my phone of any emotions that I feel for a lasting time each day, whether that be content, calm, productive, frustrated, angry, bored, tired – anything. Then I write down why, when or what has created that emotion.

It could be;

Tired – went to bed at 11pm last night, tonight needs to be a 10pm finish!

Productive – by 10am I replied to all my emails and wrote another 10 pages for this book. (it was actually 10:02 but who's watching!).

This is a great, quick way to track your emotions and start to take notice of them and what could have caused them for you.

2. Outdoors

Equipment needed

• You

Being outdoors makes a huge difference.

In every day you should spend 60 seconds just stood outside, breathing. No phone. No people. No conversation. No travelling. No direction.

60 seconds just breathing, outdoors.

Try it!

3. Intention setting

Equipment needed

- Your mind
- Commitment
- Clarity

Have you ever wondered why getting up at 3am for a holiday is never as bad as getting up at 6am to your alarm for work?

Before you go to bed each night, simply set an intention for the day ahead.

- What would you like to get done?
- How would you like to feel?
- Who would you like to speak to?

Be really clear with yourself on how you want to feel when you wake up. This creates focus, purpose and positive intention and will stop you always focussing on 'being so tired' or 'I can't believe it's time to get up already.'

4. Schedule 'You Time'

Equipment needed

- You

When living with anxiety it can create habits.

Always needing to be busy and never be alone.

Only wanting to be alone and just hide.

This tip is vital for either of these people and whichever you relate to most.

If you HAVE to be around people all the time, and fill any empty day or evening with plans, then you need to schedule time to be alone.

You have to get used to your own company and being brave enough to just be with yourself and your thoughts. This time will become your sanctuary, once you learn how to manage yourself, your thoughts and your emotions – and that can't happen if you constantly fill your time with people and plans.

If you prefer spending time alone, away from people and having to be on 'top form' all the time, away from the pressures of 'looking ok to the world.' You need to schedule time to see people and stick to those plans. Cutting yourself off from the world will only make it harder when you have to get back out in it.

Schedule a dinner date with a friend once every 2 weeks, or a DVD night with your friends once a month – AND STICK TO IT.

You need to step out of the habits you have created to keep yourself safe and start to step out of your comfort zone because – nothing changes if you change nothing and doing what you are doing now, is not healthy or sustainable for you long term. You need time with people and to interact, but you also need time alone with yourself. Balance is key – start creating it with scheduling time.

5. Positivity Party

Equipment needed

- You
- Your loved ones (if you choose them!)
- TV, Radio, Phone
- Bath tub (if baths make you happy!)
- Food

We all have things that automatically make us smile or feel warm and happy inside. It could be a film, a song, a place, a meal, a person. Think of yours now.

> **My positivity party would include;**
>
> 1.
>
> 2.
>
> 3.

Hold a positivity party as often as you need one.

Listen to your favourite song everyday on the way to work. Make it your alarm clock!

Watch your favourite film or scenes before bed or at the weekend.

Call your positivity party friend or text them when you need a boost.

Honestly – invite these positive aspects of your life in, as often as you possible can.

I spent a lot of time doing what I thought I *should* be doing or what people would *expect* me to be doing. As soon as I focused on what, who and when I felt happiest, I made these my new habits.

6. Declutter

Equipment

- You
- Time!

Having chaos and clutter surrounding you will make it harder to feel calm and in control. Decluttering is my favourite thing to do!

- If you haven't worn it in 6-12 months – donate the item to charity

- If you haven't read or looked back over the pages in 6-12 months – donate to charity

- Clear out your kitchen cupboards (you don't need 6 cans of beans 'just in case')

- Get rid of old gym trainers when you have new ones (you don't need a spare pair!)

- Perfume – use up the last drops and buy a new one

- Underwear – treat yourself and throw away the old knickers (you don't need more than 1 pairs of 'period pants')

- If someone has given you a new number – delete the old one they won't use it again

- Delete messages, emails, texts that you don't need anymore

- Remove and unfriend people on social media that you haven't seen in real life for over 12 months (unless they now live abroad!)

Honestly, I do this regularly with my Facebook community. If I read an amazing book but won't read it again, I do a giveaway in my group and send it to a new home. You can join my community and get involved in the giveaway action too.

www.facebook.com/AHappyMind1 and click on the group linked to the business page.

Decluttering is so refreshing and just gives you a new found sense of ahhhhhh! So get the rubbish bags out and start decluttering your space and life – seriously.

CHALLENGE TIME

I am here to hold you to account!

If you have an Instagram I want you to send me before and after photos in your stories and tag @a.happy.mind with the hashtag #bookdeclutterchallenge

If you're on Facebook, post your before and after shots in my group and use the hashtag #bookdeclutterchallenge

OR

Email me at

ahappymind@outlook.com

This is another call to action and remember this book needs your commitment, so get committing and show me the magic you create!

Digging Deeper

Part 2

TRIGGERS

I don't know very much about odds, but I am going to say that you have already heard this big buzz word before. If I am right, please let me know (www.facebook.com/AHappyMind1) because I think it would be fun to actually keep track of how many people have heard the word 'trigger' and how many variations there are for this buzz word!

Triggers.

I am going to talk about this in a whole new way. A way that actually makes sense and actually relates to you and where you're at!

Why do people mention triggers so much Sam?

My answer to this will never change and is something I rave about in my Facebook group – if you aren't in it, you need to come and join the family. Like yesterday!

AWARENESS.

The biggest step you will take on this self-development journey and in changing your life for the better, is awareness. Without awareness it will be almost impossible to make any changes stick, because you just won't quite know why you are doing them.

'Awareness unlocks doors you didn't even know were closed'

The tasks we will cover in this chapter are going to give you;

- Awareness
- Personal relevance
- Understanding
- Reasoning

Behind the triggers you experience and the impact these triggers really have on your life, relationships, confidence and everyday experiences.

1. Gaining awareness of the triggers you experience;

Anxiety is an emotion, like any other, and therefore there will be warning signs before the anxiety hits in full swing.

For example, if you felt nervous, you may have a warning sign of butterflies in your tummy or a dry mouth. If you felt scared, you may first become restless or fidgety. If you felt sad, before you cry, you may have an empty feeling in your tummy or an ache in your heart.

These are warning signs, just like anxiety will give you warning signs.

These are the initial 'triggers.'

Your warning signs can present themselves in 3 main ways;

Physical

Heart racing, headache, dizziness, tense shoulders, red face, butterflies, stomach ache, needing to go the toilet all the time, sweating, dry mouth – to give you an idea.

Emotional

Shy, quiet, introverted, internal questioning, doubt, fear, crying, petrified of failure or something going wrong, wanting to hide – again, to give you the basis of what emotional triggers would be defined as.

Circumstantial

Wanting to stay in the same place or space, not wanting change, refusing to get on the train or get in the car, crowds, queues, hot or cold weather, being in a waiting room, public speaking – some examples of circumstantial triggers my clients and community have expressed and explained to me and some of which could be similar too, if not the same, as your circumstantial triggers.

To become more aware, you will need to start with reflecting and focussing on where and how the anxiety presents itself and grows for you. Everyone is different and like I said, this book is here to become personal to YOU and YOUR experiences, so use this next task to help unpick the triggers YOU experience.

It is important that you think about the triggers from the smallest of changes in your mood, body or environment and work up to the warning signs that really impact you. There will always be a starting point, something small that happens that kick starts the next signal, a bit like dominoes, there will always be that first domino that needs to fall first.

Physical

Emotional

Circumstantial

You may find that all of the triggers you experience are physical. That is absolutely fine. There is no right or wrong or 'best fit' this is about awareness and becoming aware of how anxiety shows up, warns you and grows on you.

Here is my example for you (because I want to be with you every step of the way and remind you that you are not an alien, nor are you alone).

For me – it was emotional first, which then spiralled into physical.

Emotional	Physical
1. This isn't going to work (self-doubt and worry)	This leads to;
2. What if this goes wrong, what if people don't like me, what if people leave me (abandonment, judgement, fear)	5. Hot, sweaty, clammy
	6. Heart racing
	7. Restless, not being able to sleep
3. No one likes me, I have no friends, I am going to be alone (catastrophize)	8. Sore tummy, cramps, constipation, IBS
	9. Weak, tired, tension headache
4. Why is it always me this happens to? (victim, crying, despair)	10. Wanting to sleep

This activity is crucial, although it may be difficult and sometimes emotional, without doing this, your awareness and level of awareness will not change or improve.

Once you become AWARE of the triggers you experience you can start to identify them and prevent them from growing and escalating.

Exactly like seeing a child whinge, you would distract them, give them a sweet, play with them, cuddle them, feed them – so they didn't cry and scream the house down!

This is what you will be able to do for yourself.

-   Become aware
-   Identify
-   Change the pattern of thought or behaviour
-   Self-pacify
-   Prevent escalation
-   Stop anxiety growing and taking over

Go back and add any more detail, depth and context to your trigger boxes because this really is the best first step and one you do not want to skim over.

2. Personal relevance

This next step made a real difference for me and something I cannot speak about enough!

The trigger boxes you have completed; we need to start to layer this information.

Think about the personal relevance they each have to your life, experiences, trauma, memories and add this in.

Emotional

1. This isn't going to work (self-doubt and worry).

    I had experienced my parents separating at a young age and my Dad dying all before the age of 16 so things going wrong were very real for me.

2. What if this goes wrong, what if people don't like me, what if people leave me. (abandonment, judgement, fear).

    My Dad passing away unexpectedly at the age of 14, my Mum moving to another country at 21, my twin brother moving to another country at 21, therefore experiencing loss and abandonment a lot in my early years.

3. No one likes me, I have no friends, I am going to be alone (catastrophize).

    My friends became my family so I always put a lot of pressure and emphasis on them, which always made me worry that if they left I would be alone.

4. Why is it always me this happens to? (victim, crying, despair).

    I felt like I had a lot to handle early on in my life and this made me feel like it would always keep happening to me.

Put your big girl pants on and start reflecting on where those triggers have personal relevance for you. This will then help us reach

3. Understanding

Anxiety is all about the fear of the unknown, lack of control and not knowing the outcome or result of something. Anxiety can cause us to focus and live in the past or worry and want to control the future, leaving very little room for the present and being in the present.

Through creating personal relevance and then gaining understanding of why these triggers are there for you, you will have something that anxiety has worked hard to stop you gaining. Control and knowing!

So if crowds are a circumstantial trigger for you and you know the personal relevance is that you got lost at the age of 5 in a big crowd on Brighton Pier, you can then understand why crowds are still an issue – the past is still coming up in your present.

Make sense?

(I am really hoping you are having your first big A-HA moment of this book right now!)

If you would like some more support with triggers, awareness and understanding you can also watch 3 10 minute videos from my anxiety masterclass here;

https://ahappymind.clickfunnels.com/anxiety

Now for the final stage of this initial process.

4. Reasoning

Anxiety often makes you feel irrational, out of control, reactive, impulsive, crazy! After completing this first reflection you will start to feel a level of awareness and understanding for yourself, that until now, may have felt like a big grey hole.

From this you can now start to reason.

You will show compassion and empathy with those you love and care about, and yet, you probably don't show yourself these 2 vital qualities often enough.

- Do you blame yourself for the anxiety?
- Say sorry to others for feeling anxious or 'ruining plans for them'
- Do you find yourself wishing you could just forget how you feel and be 'normal'?

Enter – reasoning!

Now that you have awareness, personal relevance and understanding, you must allow reasoning to enter your thought space.

It is time to get really personal and talk to your inner most being.

Emotional

5. This isn't going to work (self-doubt and worry)

   I had experienced my parents separating at a young age and my Dad dying all before the age of 16 so things going wrong were very real for me.

6. What if this goes wrong, what if people don't like me, what if people leave me (abandonment, judgement, fear)

   My Dad passing away unexpectedly at the age of 14, my Mum moving to another country at 21, my twin brother moving to another country at 21, therefore experiencing loss and abandonment a lot in my early years

7. No one likes me, I have no friends, I am going to be alone (catastrophize)

   My friends became my family so I always put a lot of pressure and emphasis on them, which always made me worry that if they left I would be alone

8. Why is it always me this happens to? (victim, crying, despair)

   I felt like I had a lot to handle early on in my life and this made me feel like it would always keep happening to me

---

This was totally out of my control and there was nothing I could have done to change that outcome.

I wish this didn't happen to me at the age of 14, but it has taught me a lesson that I am so thankful for now.

Start to reason with those triggers, the experiences and the trauma and write a lesson to yourself, letting go of all the pain and blame you place on yourself daily.

These prompts were super helpful for me when I wrote my first letter and I really hope they can help you find the compassion and empathy for yourself, that you so rightly deserve.

Phrases of Compassion;

It is OK to have felt scared of abandonment, you experienced so much as a young person but now you can choose to see things differently. The people in your life now, are not the same people that left.

Always remember that you did the best you could, with the knowledge you had. You did the best you could and you should be so proud of yourself for that.

So let's go back to the beginning for a moment.

Every emotion has its warning signs, some are just more prominent and powerful than others.

Now that you know and understand the warning signs for the emotion anxiety, you will be able to identify when they are warning you and make the decision of;

- Is this based on my present situation or emotion?

Or

- Is this emotion based on a situation from my past and the anxiety is reminding me of that?

In simple terms;

- Is this emotion and warning sign HELPFUL or HINDERING?

Once you know this, the reasoning process can begin.

Dear ....,

Never forget that

Always remind yourself that

It was OK to feel

Now you can choose to

Now can you see why commitment is in your toolkit for this book! Being able to successfully complete this process and see real progress with take, what I call, the 3 P's;

Patience

My husband would tell you that I am the least patient person he knows! I find it so hard to wait for things, be late to events, stand in long queues with no end in sight, walk slowly behind the person just sauntering along (are you like this too?)

Two things I learnt on my own self-development journey;

1. Nothing worth having will come easy, but if it is truly worth it, you will trust the process.

2. Time changes everything – good and bad. Give yourself time to heal, time to be better, time to do better, time to feel better. Time changes everything and learning to love time, rather than want to rush through it, changed my life for the better.

You are only human and there will be hiccups and learning curves along the way, but be patient with yourself.

Persistence

One word my loved ones would use to describe is persistent. I will never ever (I mean ever) give up. If I have an idea, a plan, a goal, I will do everything I can to make that happen and I won't stop until

I know I have given it 110%.

This quality got me through a lot during my growth and I want this to become something you treasure.

Remember;

This is YOUR life. YOUR happiness. YOUR journey.

Without you, things cannot and will not change. (Hence, number 3 of your toolkit!)

Be persistent in your pursuit for happiness and the life you deserve, because you deserve the world and more – and THAT will take persistence my friend.

'Without you, things cannot & will not change'

PURPOSE

Anxiety has a great way of making you feel worthless, insignificant, strange, isolated, crazy, alone – take your pick of these words or add you own to the list. Ultimately, anxiety does not fill you with warm fuzzies and excitement, or the urge to get out of bed and jump around with enthusiasm. I want to change this for you and remind you of bigger things in your life that truly matter, rather than focus on an emotion that's main aim is to bring you down.

So, remember your 'why'.

•   Why did you buy this book?

•   Why do you want to change your life?

•   Why is overcoming anxiety important to you?

•   Why does any of this matter to you?

Use that to motivate and fuel you. Your 'why' is everything and it gives purpose to everything you will do with me in this book and everything you will continue to do after you have read the final page. Never forget your 'why'.

When anxiety tries to bring you down or stop you in your tracks, just focus on your 'why' and remind yourself of the real reason you want to believe in more than just the emotion. You deserve to believe in yourself – not an emotion that comes and goes when it pleases.

Answer these questions again to reinforce just how important purpose is for you;

- Why did you buy this book?

```
┌─────────────────────────────────────────┐
│                                         │
│                                         │
│                                         │
│                                         │
└─────────────────────────────────────────┘
```

- Why do you want to change your life?

```
┌─────────────────────────────────────────┐
│                                         │
│                                         │
│                                         │
│                                         │
└─────────────────────────────────────────┘
```

- Why is overcoming anxiety important to you?

```
┌─────────────────────────────────────────┐
│                                         │
│                                         │
│                                         │
│                                         │
└─────────────────────────────────────────┘
```

- Why does any of this matter to you?

```
┌─────────────────────────────────────────┐
│                                         │
│                                         │
│                                         │
│                                         │
└─────────────────────────────────────────┘
```

FACTS AND FEELINGS

Now we have changed your perception of the triggers you experience, gained awareness and understanding of them, the next step is to dig even further into your feelings. Yep – big girl pants are needed again!

Have you ever heard the saying 'what you focus on, expands'?

Well its true! The more you think something, the more it comes into your reality.

This was originally what I had written to start this chapter, but for the next 3 days I just couldn't continue!

So here is what I REALLY want to tell you!

Your feelings are your feelings and I am not here to say that they are good, bad, ugly or indifferent. What I am here to do, is to get you thinking about which feelings you are having that serve and support you, and which feelings you have that just poison and derail you.

We all have thoughts and feelings and these feelings can create a confident, happy, secure you OR create an insecure, doubtful and negative you.

Which type of you do you want to be?

I used to think that what I thought about in my head and the feelings I had were 100% true and therefore I had to act and believe them. I am here to tell you that you have a CHOICE. A very big, juicy, important and valuable choice.

I know how much a thought can whip up into a storm inside your mind, from a tiny little rain drop. You have the power and the choice to create the storm, live in the middle of the storm and get totally annihilated by it, or get out your umbrella and walk on by under shelter. Right now, you might be thinking 'if only it was that easy Sam, but these thoughts are all consuming.' My first response to you is 'how?'

How are they all consuming? When you have that first little raindrop thought, how does it grow and grow? Are you focusing on it? Do you sit and fester on it? Do you feed it? Are you giving it more attention than you would any other thought that pops into your mind?

Why? What about THIS thought holds an emotional attachment or insecurity for you?

Where? Where does it come from? Deep inside there will be a reason that your mind clings onto this thought and feeling, clings onto it as the truth and believes it.

This is the first process you can use to start to unpick this little rain drop and start to get your umbrella ready. You don't have to sit in the storm and feel helpless, you can become prepared and equipped to handle the down pour – trust me!

Questioning is vital. Exactly what I have just done for you, you can start to do for yourself. Get asking and get answering! Whether that be in a journal, internally, out loud in the car – it's totally your call.

You can also take me with you and listen to me in your ear with my Podcast episode 'what to do when you feel like giving up.' I share affirmations, statements and calming techniques to ensure you feel equipped and not helpless to these thoughts and feelings. (iTunes A Happy Mind in case you weren't sure!)

After questioning, you will be able to break down the thought or feeling with a more detached view and rational focus, which is where my simple flow chart comes in for you. The biggest shift that you need to make, is the ability to control the weather (metaphorically) and after answering these questions which is focussed around reflecting, this next step is all about action.

Like everything in this book, I want you to be able to screen shot this, use it, make the most of it and it actually impact your way of thinking from RIGHT NOW.

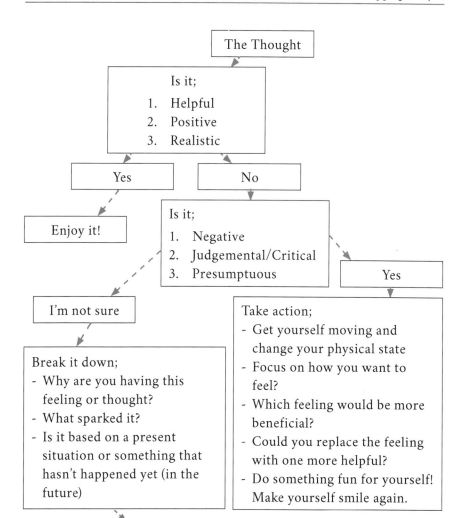

The Thought

Is it;
1. Helpful
2. Positive
3. Realistic

Yes

No

Enjoy it!

Is it;
1. Negative
2. Judgemental/Critical
3. Presumptuous

Yes

I'm not sure

Take action;
- Get yourself moving and change your physical state
- Focus on how you want to feel?
- Which feeling would be more beneficial?
- Could you replace the feeling with one more helpful?
- Do something fun for yourself! Make yourself smile again.

Break it down;
- Why are you having this feeling or thought?
- What sparked it?
- Is it based on a present situation or something that hasn't happened yet (in the future)

Take a break from the thought
- Journal it out
- Listen to your favourite song
- Enjoy something else that brings you joy until you have the clarity you need

This really is the best piece of advice I can give you on stopping your feelings becoming facts if they do not serve you.

So often we beat ourselves up about situations, people, what we have done or not done, said or not said, what we want to change, how we could have changed something and then list goes on.

Let me stop you right here and give you a little NEWSFLASH.

You are doing the very best you can, right now, in this moment.

THAT is a fact and THAT is what counts. So use this flow chart above to start taking back the awareness of your feelings and thoughts and when you may need to take action to stop them from taking over for you.

Having the feeling 'I am not good enough' is not a fact, it's a feeling and one that you will have to take action on to change and move past.

Some statements I know you will have said to yourself (because by now I know you, your face from the selfie challenge, your personality from joining my community) and let's face it, if you're reading this, I just know! These statements are something I want to help you break down a little more. Repetition and consistency make all the difference in self-development and you can never have too many practical tips and strategies – so I am going to continue to give you absolutely everything I can to change your life (I hope that's ok!).

Current statement	Positive alternative thought/ feeling
I am not good enough	I am doing EVERYTHING I can, with what I have right now – and that IS ok
People will judge me	The right people will always love and support me – focus on those people
It will go wrong, just like everything else	This is a new opportunity and a fresh opportunity
I wish I was more confident	I will not compare myself to others, my qualities are unique and amazing to me
Nothing ever goes right for me	My past does not make my present, let's make today different

Have a go for yourself – write any current statements you would like to shift.

This may sound airy fairy and wishy washy BUT the more commitment (from your toolkit) the more you engage with WHY you are reading this (again – in your toolkit) the more impact this will have on your beliefs and mind-set.

Telling yourself the current statements isn't making you feel great, or love yourself, so why not try the new positive statements and allow yourself to make a simple, yet effective change for yourself?

Remember – if you change nothing, nothing will change.

These statements do not serve or support you, so you need to start using new ones. Hence this very simple list to get you started.

Become emotionally invested in this, like I know you will, and these statements will be a game changer for you. An instant shift in your mind-set and that quick boost of positive energy you need to stop getting sucked in by the false feelings.

Say these statements to yourself daily, even when you don't feel negative or doubtful.

'I am doing everything I can, with what I have right now, and that IS ok'.

Say it right now 5 times. Listen to your voice when you say it and listen to your tone. Say it with conviction, meaning and emotion.

You are doing your very best. I know that. You just need to hear it within yourself and start believing it.

'I AM DOING EVERYTHING I CAN, WITH WHAT I HAVE RIGHT NOW, AND THAT IS OK'.

Never underestimate the power of your mind and the thoughts you create. If you need to re-read this chapter, do it. I used to hate it when I would read that because I would always think 'I just want to get to the end!'

No, no, no! I have written this book to have no end. I want to continue to be with you everywhere you go in life and I want this book to become another best friend to you. A source of guidance, honesty and advice. So the more you read this book, the more you will grow, learn and thrive.

Enjoy every chapter as many times as you need to, take notes, add notes, highlight, screen shot pages and tag me on your Insta Story or Facebook – we are friends now remember! Don't hold back! Spam away and harass my social media as much as you want to (which I hope you do!)

'I am doing the best I can, and that is OK'

PAST, PRESENT, FUTURE

I have typed, deleted and typed and deleted this first sentence 5 times. I am not saying that for any effect or impact, I want to be 100% transparent with you. One thing I always promise my social media community and Podcast listeners is that I will be;

- Real
- Honest
- Genuine

This book will be no different to that. I promise to always be 100% truthful with you – good, bad and ugly. I don't want this book to become 'just another self-development' book that you read and put on the shelf. My passion for this book is to truly help and serve you on a deeper level than any other.

So here I am, telling you I have struggled to write this first page because, on my journey with anxiety, these three words held so much power over me and my emotions.

The past was full of loss and heartbreak for me. Filled with experiences I spent a long time running from, or pretending they didn't hurt as much as they did.

The past is filled with struggle for me. Of course I had amazing memories and fun times and things I will always hold dear to my heart, but the big things, the really influential and pivotal times in my past are weighted heavily with pain, grief, disappointment, loneliness and struggle.

When starting my business from just an Instagram account, this was all because I wanted my present and future to be filled with goodness. Happiness. Hope. Love. Sunshine. So I took it into my own hands to create that for myself.

This decision only came from a place of sadness and heartache, and once again, I was being pulled back into the past. Pulled back into the person I used to be, the thoughts I used to have, the emotions I used to battle with.

- 'Why is it always me?'
- 'When will I get a break?'
- 'Why is nothing easy for me?'
- 'Am I supposed to always struggle before I find happiness and triumph?'
- 'How much more can I take?'
- 'I have had my time, please let this just work out how I want it to.'

This was the past me. A young adult that was used to being a fighter, being a survivor, being my own champion and drudging my way through things with grit in my teeth and determination in my blood. But just once, I wanted things to fall in my lap and just happen how I imagined. I wanted to click my fingers and be given a break – just a little luck!

People would say to me 'the toughest lessons are only given to those strong enough to take them' and I would constantly think, I don't want to have to be strong anymore.

So this has lead me here. On this page with you.

I know how life changing, traumatic and painful the past can be and I also know just how much this pain can continue to affect your present and actually stop your future from being any different.

This stops now.

Honestly. No more. This is not the present and future I want for you and I know it is not the present and future you want for yourself.

Being honest is never a bad thing and after worrying about how to start this chapter off with you, my honesty has created over 500 words of pure truth and that in itself is liberating. Now it is going to be your turn.

'Until you accept your past, your future will forever be tainted'

So let's stick with the past for a little longer, whilst I take you through this three step process.

1. Accountability
2. Release your past self
3. Forgiveness

If you are thinking 'what does this have to do with anxiety?' remember step 1 of your toolkit (big girl pants) and step 3 (commitment). Anxiety is fuelled by your fears, your experiences, your trauma and it grows from all of this pain. The only way to truly overcome anxiety, is to first overcome the experiences that lay deep within your past. Hence – the big girl pants!

1. Accountability

This may sound harsh (big girl pants!) but you will need to take account for how you allow yourself to feel. Over the years, and in my personal experiences, I feel I am now in a situation where I can say this to you and really talk right to your heart.

Just because something bad may have happened, it does not mean you have to feel bad all of the time. You are going to need to take accountability for the emotions you allow yourself to feel, on a regular basis, that do NOT make you happy. These choices are YOURS and no one else's.

To break it down further for you;

When my Mum moved abroad and I was in my final year of university, with no family home, no support system from parents and completely making it in the world as a full blown adult, paying bills (and still trying to be a teenager basically,) I could have chosen to give in and be beaten by circumstance.

Yes, I had down days and days of wishing things would work out, but then I dusted myself off and carried on, (bounce-back-ability is later in the book) because I could choose how I wanted to move forward. I was with myself 24/7 and how did I want to make myself feel? Continually crappy and defeated or motivated to make things better?

Whatever circumstance you find yourself in, become a go-getter and take accountability for the decisions you have made, that have kept you in the low place you may find yourself in now, and know that with a slice of awareness and a new decision, you can and will change your outlook instantly.

One thing you must know; accountability is not blame. Accountability is being strong enough to know when you have been helping yourself or hindering your progress and using that knowledge to make changes. Remember – awareness is vital and once you become aware of the choices you are making and the way you are choosing to feel, you will be able to choose again and re-set the day with your own decisions.

We will go deeper into self-talk later but for now let's start with the basics, to get this accountability party started!

What do you say to yourself that is harmful not helpful?

List as many statements or thoughts that you repeat to yourself regularly.

> For example;
>
> 'Nothing ever goes my way'
>
> 'I'm just not clever enough'

Now it is time to;

- Take account for them
- Know that you can choose again
- Make new thought habits

Now spend some time re-thinking those thoughts and how you can turn them into being helpful to you, rather than continue to be harmful.

This is what taking account is all about. Being responsible for how you want to feel and making that your focus – instead of the circumstance.

Old thought habits	New thought habits
'Nothing ever goes my way'	'What can I do to make this better? What could I try?'

2. Release your past self

In order for you to truly enjoy and thrive in your present life, you must be able to let go of the past you.

I never used to understand this, until I actually started to do the work.

When I found myself in situations of stress, conflict, judgement, fear, abandonment, (and the rest!) my younger self would always get involved and re-tell all of my past struggles to me.

'See, it is happening again. You'll always be the one who gets left'.

Past	Present	Future
Insecure about relationships – friends and boyfriends	100% happy and secure with my husband and trust him and my loved ones more than ever – I know who my support network truly is and I am happy with that	Love life together!
Constantly people pleasing and saying yes to everything and everyone	I have fewer friends and enjoy spending time alone, as well as with my friends and husband. I won't say yes to things unless I really want to – if anything I say no more!	Nurture my truest relationships and hold them close
Having to be the best at everything to prove my own self-worth and abilities	I do my best, for me, at that time, and that is good enough – I know I work hard and that's what counts	Continue to stay in my lane
Say sorry for everything because I didn't want anyone to leave me or judge me	If I feel content in my choices, I won't apologise for that anymore	Be bold enough to speak in public arenas and inspire other women everywhere
Jealous of girls talking to my boyfriend, what if they are more fun than I am	I love Luke and I trust him with my life – I know he thinks I'm the best thing since sliced bread!	Create a future of our dreams together and travel the world when we want to

Confident in my own abilities	Confident in my own abilities	Continue to stretch myself to achieve greatness
Motivated and self-driven	Motivated and self-driven	Set higher aspirational targets
Efficient with my time and always organised	Efficient with my time and always organised	Efficient with my time and always organised
Loyal to people that I love and trust	Loyal to people that I love and trust	Loyal to people that I love and trust
Wear my heart on my sleeve	Wear my heart on my sleeve	Wear my heart on my sleeve – to impact others and show they can achieve and be whatever they want to be and still be genuine

I wanted to change that and I wanted to change the way I viewed my present self. I didn't want to always feel like the victim of circumstance or other people's decisions, so I started to work on my younger self and identify the strengths I had learnt, but more importantly, identify the weaknesses I had developed, so I could work through them and no longer be held back by them.

Living in the past, or living with the past as a constant burden will continually pull you back and bring you down and anxiety will LOVE that! Anxiety will literally relish in this insecurity and continually remind you of these weaknesses when any hardship comes your way, just amplifying how you have felt before and make you keep feeling that way.

Awareness is a running theme for this book and your big girl pants will get very used to looking inward and reflecting on where you are and where you want to be, plus how you actually get there.

During this next task I want you to take as much time as you need and use my prompts to help guide you through each stage. I will give you exactly what I give my 1:1 coaching clients and break this task down in exactly the same way.

The above table is mine and I think it highlights to you, just how much you can change your life and grow as a person, when you have the right tools, support and commitment.

My past column is not who I am now and I have worked tirelessly to become my present self. This transformation and growth is what I want for you, I don't want you to be locked in the past and cooped up in the thoughts of what has already happened, therefore missing out on what is happening now and what amazing things are waiting for you in the future. This next task is designed to allow you to see just how your past has been holding you back from who you want to be and provide you with the next steps, the tools to get to the best present you, you can be and to be able to really thrive in your future – without the past baggage weighing you down.

The future column is where I want to get to, what I am for in myself and in my life, who I want to continue to become.

When completing your table, focus on the past and future column and then the present column is what we will focus on. How you get from past you, to future you and the steps you can take to get there.

Your past self has to be laid bare. Be brutally honest with how your past self affects and impacts your life. What does she stop you from doing, stop you from feeling, keep you from, hold you back, restrict you, judge you – how does your past self, control who you are in the present and who you will become in the future.

Unless you are crystal clear with your future self, your present self cannot work towards getting you there.

Once you have your past column and your future column, we need to let go of your past self. You did the best you could, in the circumstance you were in and did what you thought you had to do at that time. BUT – the past doesn't have to continue to talk to you now.

You know more, understand yourself better, have more awareness of your emotions and thoughts, have the tools to make change happen. Therefore, your past self doesn't need to keep worrying that you won't be ok now.

With that in mind, think about which aspects of your past self are helpful to you and therefore you want to continue to grow and develop, and identify which aspects have been holding you back, which present and future you no longer need.

Past	Present	Future

I was asked yesterday on a client call

'Sam, how did you do it?'

There are two words that instantly popped up for me.

- Clarity
- Consistency

Clarity – you have to really *see* your future self in your mind. What does she look like? Dress like. Behave like. How does she hold herself? Who are her friends? What are her hobbies? What makes her laugh? What does she steer clear of? When does she relax and how?

Literally everything.

I created an avatar of my future self and worked relentlessly to embody this best version of myself.

Reading this book isn't enough. Which is why I have been asking you to take constant action with your thoughts and tasks here too.

This is no different. Your future self needs to be engrained in your mind, so that present self can take small steps every day to become the person you always wanted to become. Little and often (which I know people say about food, but I say it about growth and development).

If your present steps can do small, tiny things every day, all the time, as often as you can, you will slowly chip away at those old habits and 'past you' thinking and evolve into your future avatar.

Honestly clarity changed the game for me.

The clearer, more specific you can be, the better it is for your mind and conscious thinking. If you can associate with this future you and emotionally invest in who that person is, you will be able to successfully embody her into your life and let go of the past you that has been there out of default and routine.

'Your future
self needs to
be engrained in
your mind'

I want you to get to know your future self!

Write around her, draw on her, stick your favourite or dream outfit on her, colour her in – whatever you need to do, to get in touch with your best self.

This is going to be you!

You will and can become your future self, she is hiding within you now – you just need to be brave enough to let her out!

CONSISTENCY

This is all about creating habits that work *for you* NOT *against you*. Self-development and your own growth all stems from consistency. The more you want this, the more you will show up for yourself. The more time you will put in. The more energy and effort you will continue to invest into your progress. The more open minded and willing you will be to create new habits and stick to them.

Consistency is showing up for yourself and showing yourself that you are the priority. If you cancel your journaling, positive self-talk, meditation, morning walk – whatever it may be, to have a lay in 4 days a week – you won't see yourself evolving into your future self any time soon.

If you change nothing, nothing will change.

Use that to fuel your consistency but also your focus. This is all about YOU and YOUR journey to happiness. YOUR journey to a future without anxiety being in charge. YOU have to put in the effort to make that happen.

Think about your habits now and how you can implement small changes from today. How can you embed more positivity, productivity, clarity, motivation, energy, into your life every single day?

Some prompts for you;

- Instead of listening to the radio on your way to work, listen to a Podcast

- Swap lyrical music for classical or melodies to relax your mind

- Use the stairs at work, instead of the lift

- Do all your clothes washing on a Sunday and declutter your week (routines are everything!)

- Go out for dinner once a week and spend the other nights at home (spending time on yourself and with yourself will become priceless)

- No takeaways in the week (what you feed your body, you feed your mind)

- Stop watching the news

- Remove all people from social media that don't make me feel good (don't let comparison-itus happen every day!)

- Take a class or course

- Go for a walk once a week and clear your mind

- Stop watching all of the soaps (4 hours of watching drama and tragedy a night – do you need this?!)

- Booking a night away from home once every 6-8 weeks

- Drinking water instead of coffee or tea at work (hydrating is vital)

- Revamp the photos in my home (seeing positive memories will affirm your positive identity)

What small things can you promise yourself, that you know will improve your life, your happiness, your mind-set daily;

Easy changes I will make;	Changes I will work toward;
1.	1.
2.	2.
3.	3.
4.	4.
5.	5.

'Nothing changes,
if you change
nothing'

BOUNCE-BACK-ABILITY

Now we have come to the end of Part 2, this is the final piece of advice I need to share with you. Before we look at the extra support for your life and also hold our positivity party!

Your bounce-back-ability!

Let's be real – because that's how I roll! You are human and not a robot. That's how we want it to stay. You are a human, who has human experiences in a human world.

You cannot control other people's actions, you cannot stop bad things happening, you cannot change outcomes that are meant to happen.

All you can do is learn how to manage your own emotions, your own thoughts and your own mind-set to always work for you not against you.

You will have heard all the famous sayings about picking yourself back up, it's not about falling it's about rising again, get knocked down 7 times, get up 8 and all the quotes in-between.

Ultimately, my message is simply this.

You are able to change and choose how you feel, in an instant.

When my Dad died at age 14, it devastated my life. Changed me as a person. Broke me. Showed me just how cruel the world could be.

Ruined me. Totally and utterly shattered my world and ripped out my heart in one hit.

At no point could I change or control this or do anything to make this outcome different, no matter how much I wish with all my might that I could. I will never stop grieving, missing him, crying when a memory hits, feel sad that he isn't here. But what I can do, is choose how this affects me.

Do I want my grief to dictate my life now? Do I want to be held back constantly because of this tragedy?

No.

I wanted to be motivated to always do him proud. I wanted to show the world that I can still succeed, I can still take everything he taught me and be my best self.

THIS is what I mean by bounce-back-ability. It's not about ignoring the bad bits or pretending they haven't happened; it's about using that in a way that you can take something good away from even the worst situations.

The reason I have shared this example with you and none of my other life changing events, is because I don't want you to think that I take this lightly or in any way think it's easy. Bouncing back is hard and takes time to learn and adjust. But I promise you, once you have put into practice all of the tools, tricks and tips so far, your life, mind and thoughts will start to change for good and you will know how you want to feel – even when the storm hits.

You'll get out that umbrella and you'll walk right out the other side.

So never forget that you can control your own outcome and you can choose how you want to feel – in ANY situation that gets thrown your way. It's just about bouncing back and getting out your umbrella!

Take some time to think about your storms and how they still impact you now. How those past events are still affecting your present and what can you do to change that?

- What lessons can you take away?
- What strength can you gain?
- How can you use this to motivate you moving forward?

Use the space below to get those storms out on paper and no longer let them hold such a huge space inside your mind and thoughts.

Specific Support

Part 3

RELATIONSHIPS

Firstly, I plan on writing a whole book all around anxiety in a relationship because I just have SO much to tell you! (This also keeps me accountable to write the next book – goals are key for our mind-set and purpose!)

So this will be our phase 1 of relationships, and the fundamentals that you need to get things moving forward positively.

Wow where do I begin! Literally, my mind works at 100 miles an hour (if I am your coach, you will know this already) if you would like me to become your coach then head over here; https://www.ahappymind.co.uk/copy-of-coaching-programs

With that in mind, it does mean that I have to make sure I don't bombard you too quickly, so just bear with me, as this is such juicy stuff, I have to keep myself in check too!

The best place to start is right now and where you are (funny that!)

I do this a lot and my husband used to say this to me a lot

'Check yourself before you wreck yourself' which he must have got from somewhere but who knows! It actually made perfect sense to me though and has inspired me to start with this quote. We all have to check in with ourselves, as regularly and honestly as possible, to stop ourselves from getting carried away in the negatives or struggles we all face.

So here is your first chance to 'check yourself' and this is where your trusted someone from your toolkit will come in most use.

This task is not;

- About blame
- About making anyone feel bad or insignificant
- Trying to point score
- Pretending

This task is about;

- Being honest
- Being open minded
- Being supportive
- Sharing good communication that is constructive
- Creating a level of understanding that you may not have had before

Stage 1;

You must complete your own reflection. What qualities do you possess that are positive, enriching and enhance your character?

Which traits do you feel you could work on or would like to improve/progress in? How do they impact you now and could working on them make your persona feel more like you and make you feel happier in yourself?

You on You	
Positives	Areas to develop

Stage 2;

Your other half does the same task on your character and is allowed to be honest and open.

This will only work if you are both honest with one another.

Sometimes we think we have a quality that we would like to improve and they actually love that about us and think it's unique and valuable. It is a great way to prevent assumption and ensure that what you want from your relationship and how you want to be in your relationship is shared openly together.

Them on You	
Positives	Areas to develop

Stage 3;

You need to let your partner/loved one know the qualities you love and appreciate about them. When anxiety kicks in, a lot of the time we will become defensive, or shut ourselves away from those we love most, which can leave them feeling helpless and uncertain of what to do. This stage is vital in expressing how you feel about your loved one but also providing them an insight into what is in your thoughts, that you may not share. You must then explain the qualities or actions that potentially trigger anxiety or cause it to grow. For example, an area I would like you to develop is to not say that "I am crazy when we have an argument because this automatically makes me want to protect myself, but also makes me feel like I am not normal and that plays on my mind".

Be honest and open with them, like they were with you and this avenue for communication and understanding will continue to grow.

You on Them	
Positives	Areas to develop

This task can be done as many times as you need to, in as much depth as you want to go with but remember, like everything in this book, the more you invest your time and energy into each activity and doing each activity whole heartedly, the more impact it will have for you.

Now you have shared, listened and respected one another's space the final stage is all about connection and sharing a way forward that means you are both on the same page.

When we are led by emotions it can be very easy to say things we don't mean, or even say things we really want to mean and stick to, but when the intensity of the emotion wears off – so does that intention or statement. Doing this task together, when both calm and rational, is the best way to agree a joint plan of action and also allow one another the time and space to really think before reacting and therefore making implementing the actions, far more likely.

Together we need to;

1.

2.

3.

4.

5.

I will focus on;

1.

2.

3.

………….. will focus on;

1.

2.

3.

We will both try not to;

1.

2.

This is a simple prompt for you to use for this final activity together. Change the numbers, add to it, complete this in a way that works for you and your relationship. Ultimately it is about;

- Agreeing a way forward together
- Sharing accountability for growth and development
- Becoming aware of both parties and not placing blame on one another
- Seeing a better future together that works for both of you
- Connecting with purpose and positivity at the forefront

Everything takes time and this is about not letting anxiety become the third wheel in your relationship anymore and you taking back that control together. When you feel like you have a shared outcome and goal, it will also alleviate the pressure for both of you to think it is all down to you to 'fix things' or 'make things better' or 'resolve the argument,' which will then also stop the guilt and blame game happening. Such an easy trap to fall into (trust me, I have been there!)

3 quick and easy strategies for you both when anxiety or conflict sets in;

Pause

Purpose

Praise

I love alliteration!

PAUSE

Before reacting, retaliating or feeding into an emotion or response to one another, just pause. The more awareness you have of your reactions, the more this will make a huge impact moving forward. You don't have to leave the conversation or walk away from the other person (if that could make things worse) you simply have to say "can I just have a minute?"

Create a pause in dialogue.

Create a pause in dialogue – I can't stress that enough.

Breaking the cycle of you said, they said, but no, that's not true, etc, etc is vital. It allows both people to have that slice of calm that their mind is not giving them.

Pause before you continue to feed and fuel the situation with more emotion, judgment or negativity.

PURPOSE

Think about the purpose. Always focus on purpose. Literally purpose needs to become your best friend!

What is the purpose of this statement?

What purpose does this reaction have?

It sounds like a lot of thinking but honestly, once you learn something that can be helpful, it will be hard for you to forget and unlearn it.

If you know that anxiety and those negative emotions creates a lot of irrational thinking and reactions, this word is even more important.

What is the purpose of what you are about to say? What do you want to happen next?

Is the statement, behaviour, reaction purposeful or purposeless?

If it is purposeless then you know you are setting your loved one up to fail because nothing they do is going to be right or good enough, because you don't have a purpose for your statement or behaviour.

Create purpose in every situation.

The purpose could be;

- To gain reassurance
- To help the other person understand your mood
- To seek clarity about a situation
- To ask for accountability
- To ease the tension

These are purposeful intentions and when you have a purpose in mind, it is always easier to reach a solution or resolution than when you have no purpose at all.

PRAISE

Once you set your shared action plan, when either person upholds their end, there must be praise. If your partner then doesn't call you crazy in the argument, but says that they need a minute, when things have calmed down simply say 'thank you for not calling me crazy.' Every action can be rewarded, acknowledge and praised. The more you do this, the more you solidify the response and make it more likely to happen again.

Praise is something we all crave as children but as adults, we so easily forget, but in this situation, praise will support what you are doing together and strengthen the progress you are making in your relationship.

Praise, praise and more praise.

Oh and by the way - not cringy, patronising praise! Just genuine thank you' s, gratitude, acknowledgment.

'Pause.
Purpose.
Praise'

TRAVELLING

This comes up a lot for my clients and community. Anxiety when travelling, going somewhere new, changing surroundings, fear for safety while travelling.

As with everything in the book I am going to provide you with hands on tips that you can take with you when you need to travel or change your surroundings.

5 Magic Moments (alliteration again!!)

1. Why?
2. Feelings of completion
3. Focus on the moment you are in

WHY?

When you have to travel somewhere, there can be a lot of variables and unknowns.

- What if I get stuck in traffic?
- What is the car breaks down?
- What if the exit is nowhere near me on the plane?
- How long will I be without fresh air and solid ground?
- Will I be able to stop for water?
- Do I have enough supplies just in case?
- What if my phone dies?

The list goes on and I have heard them all from clients, my community and loved ones. These anxieties and worries are the fears we create in our mind, of things that haven't happened yet.

The key thing to remember here is, the worries are based around things that haven't happened yet and may not ever happen – the unknown.

So your WHY is priceless. Your 'why' must give you the solid foundation and motivation to get yourself moving and not turning back.

Even if it is simply getting petrol, without travelling in your car, you could not get petrol, which could therefore mean you cannot commute to work.

Every journey you do or set out to do, focus on your 'why' first.

Travelling has never been a huge trigger of anxiety for me, but it can trigger a lot of resistance for me sometimes. If I have to travel into London on the train, during rush hour or home during rush hour, I instantly think of the crowds, the heat, not having enough room or a seat to sit on.

So when I think of my 'why', it is always enough to push me through.

This is a great example!

A few weeks ago I attended an amazing women's conference but it finished at 5pm, which meant I would be travelling home from London Waterloo at bang on rush hour time!

I then couldn't get on the underground for the one stop back to Waterloo – delays (if you use the underground you will know this struggle!) plus it was also 28 degrees – yep, sweat central for me! My wedges were now cutting my feet and seriously uncomfortable, bring on the limp!

So now I am walking to Waterloo, sweaty and with blisters! But when I got to Waterloo, it was quiet! A train was waiting to leave in 6 minutes and I got a seat straight away.

The 'why' was huge for me – I wanted to get home and start my weekend, so I powered on and I was pleasantly surprised.

Start with your 'why' and let that lead the way – instead of the unknowns and things that haven't happened yet. No matter what does or doesn't happen, by travelling you will reach or achieve your 'why' and THAT needs to be your driving force.

FEELING OF COMPLETION

My second favourite tool is all about the end result. No traffic can last forever. No crowd stays put. Everything ends and changes, just like time, the weather, emotions, seasons, programmes.

So for me focussing on the end outcome is always a great driver for me, and for my clients.

Focus on how you will feel once you have COMPLETED the journey.

- Pride
- Relief
- Happiness
- Calm
- Confidence
- Achievement
- Success
- Growth
- Resilience

Whenever you complete or do something that you find challenging, the positive feelings that follow will outweigh the anxious feeling or thoughts that you experienced.

The illation of driving on your own for the first time, even if it is round the block, or getting on a plane with your family for the first time in 10 years, or a train to go away with your partner for a special occasion – doing all of those things and reaching the end result and saying 'I did that!' is powerful.

Focus on that. Focus on how you WILL feel when you achieve something great for yourself. Focus on the moment you can turn around and say

'have that anxiety – I did it anyway!'

Honestly, if I could bottle that up for you now and give you a slice of the magic I would.

The first time I felt that, I just wanted more of it. The pleasure I felt in being able to have a taste of freedom from the anxiety was exhilarating and from then on, I wanted to do all I could to keep moving in that direction. Progress.

If this process is brand new for you (which I think it will be, because you haven't read this book with me before!) Then let's take a moment to do the following;

Whatever it is that creates the fear, the anxiety and the doubt for you, wherever it takes you in your mind, or how it makes you feel, try these simple tasks.

- Write down your 'why'
- Go back to the purpose, the intention
- Write down how you WANT to feel afterwards
- What would you say to your present self now?

- If this was your best friend, loved one, child – what would you say to them?
- How would you reassure them?

These are your starting points, your prompts. If you were to speak to me on the phone and we had 1:1 coaching, these are some of the simple techniques I would share with you.

So next time you need this – try it in here with me. I am here with you. You are not alone and this WILL be ok.

Write down your 'why'

Go back to the purpose, the intention

Write down how you WANT to feel afterwards

What would you say to your present self now?

If this was your best friend, loved one, child – what would you say to them?

How would you reassure them?

Answer these questions out loud, in your head, on this paper as often as you need to.

Little steps often are key and this is the first simple step, to gaining back control of your thoughts and how you want to feel and not letting anxiety butt in and ruin things all the time!

CHANGE

WOW – this is huge for me and to be honest, is probably why it is the final chapter of part 3!

I used to always find change really difficult to accept and also to handle. I wanted everything to stay the same, be how they have always been and remain constant, just how I had gotten used to it. When things changed, I always felt on the back foot, like I was having to respond to the change and just felt really unsettled.

When I look back and reflect now, I know that this is because I experienced so much change as a young person. Change that was huge, out of my control and also extremely devastating. So change for me never meant a good thing!

I told you that I want to be there for you every step of the way and that this book wasn't just a book, but to become your best friend and I think the best way to do that, is to always be open and vulnerable with you. Not for sympathy, but to give you empowerment and the encouragement that you can get through it too and no situation is ever given to you, without you being strong enough to overcome it.

At age 7 my parents separated and my Mum moved out of the family home and I become the women of the house. I would make my brother and I school lunches, help iron my school uniform and my Dad's work shirts and generally become a help around the house. I knew no different so this extra responsibility, for me, was normal. By the time I reached my teenage years, I was very protective of my brother (although we argued like twins do at that age) I loved him senseless and would do anything I could to protect him and make sure he was protected from the sadness and hurt I could see around us, as well as the conflict that still lived between our parents.

My Dad then, as you already know, died unexpectedly at age 14. This was a change I can never truly explain and can honestly only describe this change as brutal and sickening.

My parents loved us both, but in their own unique ways, as all parents do. So when our Mum moved home, this change was huge. A new family dynamic and new relationships to manage and build.

When my Mum then met someone new and moved away, there was more change for us which involved people leaving and life taking another massive turn.

Along all of these hardships, there were amazing times, of course, but ultimately I am here to be frank with you and I cannot lie and say that things were peachy all the time, because they weren't.

Relationships became fractured and my early twenties were filled with insecurity and frustration.

One vivid memory I have was at my 21st birthday party, when the boys had to wear blue and the girls had to wear pink (classic battle of the sexes for us as twins!) and I remember sobbing my heart out on a friend's shoulder. Crying like all of my heartache had been locked up for the past 6 years. That loud wailing cry you do when it just cannot be any worse. Yep, that was me, in the middle of the night club, on my 21st birthday.

So it is clear to say that change has not been a friend to me in my early years and is something I went on to fear and absolutely dread if I'm honest.

I associated change with loneliness, anger, disappointment and heartache.

Even a simple thing, like a friendship dynamic changing or 2 friends meeting without me, would panic me.

- Am I getting forgotten?
- Am I going to be left behind?
- Do they still like me?

I know you will have felt this way, in one form or another. It may not be loss, or death but it may be around a traumatic event or something sudden and this has sparked off a negative association to change.

This is what we are here to break down for you my lovely.

That's right!

No more fear.

No more dread.

No more insecurity.

Change will no longer be your enemy and I am going to show you how and why!

This may be the hardest challenge so far, because it is so deep rooted, but it may also then become the most powerful asset and tool you learn, so be open, get your big girl pants ready and let's get going.

Start here;

Why does change affect me?

What am I afraid will happen?

What is the worst case scenario when change occurs?

How will I be made to feel?

What does change mean to you and your life?

This may not quite flow, but it is something I know I have to share with you right here and now.

Blame, guilt and shame.

3 words loaded with negativity and struggle.

When you think about the changes you have experienced in your life, that have lead you to feel the way you do now, is there any element of blame, guilt or shame attached?

If I am brutally honest with you now, and I don't talk about this often, but for you, I know it is needed.

I spent years blaming myself for my Dad dying. I didn't go with him to Tesco when he had his first fall 2 years before he died and he had stitches in hospital. I called his phone because I just knew and he answered from the ambulance. This happened again a year later and I just knew. That gut feeling. I just knew. I called my Mum to explain how I felt, and as I did, the police knocked on my door and I was right. He had fallen again. So my Dad being unwell or in pain, I felt so much guilt for him falling and used to think that if I was there I could have caught him, held him up, stopping it from happening.

I felt shame when my Mum first left, like it was our fault and we weren't good enough. Which I know now wasn't the case, but I felt shame. I was on my own at 21 and that was a tough pill to swallow.

I took all of this blame, guilt and shame into any new situation that involved change. I carried it with me.

So if my 2 friends did meet without me, it was instantly because I had done something wrong, I wasn't fun enough, liked enough. I blamed myself and felt that same shame I felt all those years ago.

Telling you this, is not only empowering and comforting for you, but a huge relief for me, that I can share this with you, in this safe space and show you just how different life can become.

So before go deeper into change, I want you to write a letter to your younger self, giving them the reassurance you craved so badly.

Tell your younger self, just what you wish you could have heard when change/trauma/sadness was present for you.

Change is hard for anyone, but for you, it may have felt even harder. Let your younger self know that you are ok, things are ok and you are changing your life now.

I'll give you a slice of my letter and I really hope you allow yourself to release what has been holding you back from the past experiences.

Sam,

Please don't worry, you will be ok, you will always be ok.

There is nothing you could have done to change the situations you were in; you were just a child. It wasn't your job to think like you do now, it was your job to be a child, a daughter, sister and friend.

Sam – you have done so well for yourself and always tried so hard to achieve what you have and your Dad will always be proud of you and love you endlessly. He loves you for everything you have achieved and the young women you grew into and you know he was with you every step of the journey.

You cannot control other people's actions and you cannot take the blame for what other people choose to do – they aren't you and you can't change that.

Just keep focusing on you hun, you are doing a great job and it's time for you to choose you for once, focus on you and your happiness, worry about you for a change and not everyone else and what they are doing.

What is done is done, replaying it, blaming, overthinking – changes nothing about it, it just brings you down.

Let it go and focus on you now.

Let go of the blame, the guilt and the shame. This is your life and remember 'you are doing the best you can, with what you have right now and that is OK'.

It doesn't have to be perfect, follow a structure, have a plan – just speak from your heart and speak directly to your younger self. What does she need to hear to move forward?

Ahhhh… what a relief.

Things change, when you change your perspective and that is exactly what this is all about. Changing the way you see yourself, changing the way you see your life and changing the way you see change! Creating a friendship with change and not an enemy.

So;

How can I use this change to better myself?

What can I learn from this change?

Is there another reason for the change, that has nothing to do with me?

Can this change benefit me? Think about this one – you'll be surprised!

```
[                                                    ]
[                                                    ]
```

Has this changed happened before? What did I do then?

```
[                                                    ]
[                                                    ]
```

Can I bounce back? (the answer is always yes to this one, it might just take you a little longer!)

```
[                                                    ]
[                                                    ]
```

The thing with change is, it's here to stay (hear me out!)

You cannot run away from things changing or stop change from happening. So along this journey together and the last few pages of compassion, understanding, growth and digging deeper, the bottom line is – learn to embrace change and use change to your advantage.

- If you see change as negative, it will become negative.

- If you see change as something to fear, when it happens you will instantly feel a need to protect yourself.

- When change is associated with hurt, pain and grief – any change will bring on those feelings.

- When your change comes to you, it's not about changing the change, it's about changing your relationship with the change.

Have you noticed how many times I have said change?! Get used to using and seeing this word like any other, it isn't a word or thing to control, it's something to become familiar with and learn to embrace.

Change is inevitable, how can you bounce-back from change? This is the question you need to focus on.

When change does happen that brings you down;

Have a pity party!

Just allow yourself some time to feel down, have your space and be with the emotions, but you must have an end point for this pity party.

Once the party is over, you must then;

- Change your state and get moving
- Focus on other aspects of your life and relationships
- Do something with meaning and purpose
- Externalise and be around your loved ones

Don't allow the change to dictate you and your emotions for too long, because you must remember, this won't change the change, it will just change how you see and feel about change.

Positivity Party!!

Part 4

BFF'S

I have saved the best until last for you! Yep – you are welcome!

You need to become your very own BFF. The more you love yourself, the more you honour yourself, listen to yourself, trust yourself, care for yourself. It sounds cheesy and trust me I have heard and seen A LOT of self-love quotes and self-care messages but this is where it is at.

The more you can love yourself, the more you will honour yourself and this is a huge part of moving past anxiety and letting go of what has been holding you back.

Because let's face it – you get used to how you feel, you get used to what your mind says to you, you get used to the conflict and the constant pull from anxiety, you learn to live with it.

THIS is what I want you to shift the most. As soon as you accept all of this for yourself, you are also accepting that you are not worth more than that. When you 1,000% are.

I would say things to myself like;

- You are just going to have to get used to being this way
- You're an anxious person and that's how it is
- You can't change this now, it's been too long

These statements are showing how much I loved myself. Not a whole lot.

I felt less than everyone else and allowed this emotion to take over my being and just accepted it.

I don't want that for you. Not in the slightest.

So before you submit and just lay down your true happiness for anxiety, let's get some love and compassion truly back into your veins!

You must use this section of the book for what is says – your very own positivity party. If you approach this with the same attitude that you have had in the past, you will continue to get the same outcome. Be open minded and willing to accept a new way of seeing yourself. That is where the magic can really begin for you.

First things first. **Your love list!**

Here is where you think about as many things that truly make you smile, feel warm inside and bring you joy.

I didn't write this book to only focus on the anxiety and negatives, but to provide solutions and positivity to your life.

This list is for all of the things you love, enjoy and make you smile, it can be people, places, food, smells, songs, scenery, colours, animals, anything and everything.

let's Kick Anxiety's Butt!

Some of mine are; my husband, sunshine, baths, food I don't have to cook, travelling, any adventure, my nieces and nephews, yellow, flip flips – I could go on and on!

1.

2.

3.

4.

5.

6.

7.

8.

9.

10.

11.

12.

13.

14.

15.

16.

17.

18.

19.

20.

This love list is now your daily reminder – are you doing these things as often as you can? Surrounding yourself with these people daily? Bringing these elements into your life frequently enough?

It is no good having a love list, if you don't love everything on it and get excited about each and every thing.

Each and every day, aim to achieve, be around, do, see, at least 3 of your love list and bring joy and happiness into your day, even if, in tiny slices, as often as you possibly can.

Have you heard the phrase 'life is what you make it?'.

Well it is! So make your day as positive as you can and do what YOU can to bring joy in.

Phase 1 of make yourself your BFF is complete. (Well if you actually bring your love list into your day it is!)

Are you ready to learn more?

This love list is the starting point to increase your awareness of the positives and divert your attention from anxiety and the negatives you may think or feel, replacing that energy and attention with good old goodly goodness!

MORNING ROUTINE

Right, first things first. You are amazing. You really are. And I want you to believe that too.

The more you hear something, the more you can resonate, the more emotion it will evoke, the more warmth it can draw in.

Loving yourself is so important and routine is a huge part of that.

When you eat, when you sleep, when you rest, when you socialise, when you journal, when you meditate. Whatever it may be, you need to create positive routines in your day that show the love and respect to yourself that you truly deserve.

If you skip meals, you are telling yourself that your health and nutrition can 'wait.' It can't.

You matter most in the world and without you loving yourself and allowing yourself to thrive, something will always be imbalanced.

When I say morning routine, I don't mean get up an extra hour early and create more jobs for you to do, I mean; make your morning work for you, not the other way round.

Some simple ideas to help you become a better self-lover;

1. Set an alarm for when you will actually get out of bed and stop pressing snooze 5 times before you get up – this tells yourself

that you aren't ready for the day and automatically puts you on the back foot and tired persona.

2. Know what you will have for breakfast the day/week before (I buy cereal at the weekend for the week) and set aside time to eat it sat down. Eating on the move, for the first meal of the day is telling yourself that you are spending today rushed and are not worthy of spending 5 minutes eating your breakfast. It doesn't take a lot to make sure you eat properly and purposefully.

If you are saying – well I commute for an hour every day on a packed train and I cannot eat breakfast unless I have it on the train.

Your mind-set is already on the defensive and not working for you, but against you.

Eat when you first get to work (I always ate my breakfast at school as a teacher and I always ate it sat down in the staff room and not in my office – the staff could vouch for that!)

If you have children, you will prepare their breakfast and they will sit and eat it, because breakfast is important and it helps get them set up right for the day. Do yourself this same courtesy and eat breakfast, sat down and calmly.

3. Do not go straight on social media. Allow your brain time to engage with your thoughts and wake up to a fresh day, before polluting it with other people's information and memes. This

is just a simple way of honouring your own thoughts and mind first and giving yourself the time to awaken.

4. Set an intention for your day. How do you want the day to work for you? What do you want to take away from today? How will you answer this question when you get home;

'So how was your day today?' Clarity and purpose are important and if you set your intention with these aspects in mind, it leaves less wriggle room for your mind to take you wondering.

5. Replacement. What can you replace for something more beneficial?
- Water for your first drink, before tea or coffee.
- Vitamins first before breakfast.
- Podcast instead of a radio station playing the same songs every morning.
- Walk instead of run to the train or bus.
- Breakfast sat down instead of on the run.
- A bath instead of a rushed shower that hasn't even warmed up.
- No snooze and one alarm clock.
- A song instead of an alarm noise waking you up.
- Gym in the morning instead of after work tired.

Your replacements are there to show yourself that you matter, you value yourself and you value your happiness and wellbeing first and foremost.

I can replace;

SELF-SABOTAGE

So now you have your love list and your morning routine covered, it's time to identify why you are not your own BFF, as much as you can be.

Anxiety has its own crafty little friend that creates excuses, doubt and every reason NOT to do something and this is called self-sabotage.

Anxiety creates a lot of knock on emotions and judgement of yourself is a big one.

Even though you know something will make you feel better or doing something will have a benefit to you, you will listen to every reason not to do it and not to take action and continue to wallow in the self-pity slump, continue to listen to the victim in your head and let the anxiety totally suck you in. When this happens, it's not about placing more judgement on yourself and getting frustrated that this has happened, its simply about awareness and knowing how you can stop self-sabotage from swooping in and making things ten times worse.

Remember, anxiety doesn't like change, doesn't like risks, doesn't like the unknown, it hates feeling out of control and in danger, which you know already. Self-sabotage is just another tactic anxiety will use to prevent you from doing something that could involve any of the above; change, risk, the unknown.

Becoming your own BFF is having the understanding, the rational, deep knowledge of what you really need. You could call this your intuition, your gut instinct but ultimately it's listening to the person deep inside you and asking her what she really wants, not what the crafty self-sabotage is telling you, you need.

- I really want to go to that party vs I need to feel safe
- I'd love to go to that big festival vs I need to know how far away it is
- Going to this networking event sounds so amazing vs I can't because I can't go alone, I would need to take someone

These are such simple examples, but you get the jist.

Identify what you would really, I mean really like to do, and focus on that. The doubts, worries and fears can never be answered by not trying, all that answers is the statement that the love you have for yourself isn't enough to trust your own true judgment.

Self-sabotage keeps you believing in the past risks and doesn't allow you to explore or experience any present or future opportunities.

Think of the film The Truman Show (classic!) Jim Carrey is convinced that the life he has is the best, most amazing life ever and he is kept in that world. Oblivious to the amazing adventures, people and places he could go, because at every turn, his current life is all he is exposed to.

Until he wakes up and takes that risk, sees life in a new and exciting way and takes the risk. Who knows if it would be better or worse, but he loved himself enough to try.

Self-sabotage is your very own Truman Show. Don't let your past experiences stop you from trying something new, or you will never know what else could enrich your life and will continue to be held back by all the 'what if's'.

If you never try, you will never know and if you don't try, you will continue to believe a false thought, rather than a real experience.

'If you don't try, you will continue to believe a false thought'

www.ahappymind.co.uk

YOUR FUTURE

You cannot be your own BFF if you don't allow yourself to have goals, aspirations, big plans for your future.

You are your biggest asset, your biggest weapon to progress, growth and success. See that within yourself and allow your mind and thoughts to focus on the positive, amazing, great things in your life and no longer be sucked into the negative, the anxiety, the fear.

Love yourself enough to choose a different outcome.

If it was your best friend, saying she just doesn't know what to do or doesn't think she can go travelling or go for the promotion or say yes to the date, you would 100% support her, love her and encourage her. It's time to do that for yourself now. You need to become your biggest cheerleader because everyone has their own life to lead and own lessons to learn, you cannot rely solely on others to give you love and guidance, give it to yourself and give it to yourself in bucket loads.

Your life is yours. No one else's. Yours. Make it as great as YOU possibly can. Make the changes and growth for YOU and YOUR happiness. This is YOUR life my lovely. YOURS.

Whose life is this? Whose eyes are reading this book? Whose hands have been writing and reflecting in this book?

YOURS.

Keep loving yourself and showing up and focus on your best life and best future, not where you were or have been.

Let's get planning!

This is one of the most empowering sessions I do with my 1:1 clients and it really does shift from lack to abundance, from risk to reward and from danger to opportunity and I want to share that magical moment with you too.

There are no limits here, no judgements, no excuses – just opportunity. You are going to think BIG. No more worrying about crafty self-sabotage, guilt, insecurity or anxiety, focus on the love you have for yourself and the life you are going to be creating. YOUR BEST LIFE.

So here's to our final steps together in this book – but remember, the journey doesn't stop here. You can connect and find me on all my social media platforms and review this book on Amazon too. (Which of course I would love, as I want as many women to know about this book and enjoy the golden nuggets inside!).

This year I will achieve;

It can be within relationships, career, mind-set, confidence, travel, hobbies – ANYTHING!

In 5 years' time I will be;

Be as bold and brave as you possibly can be. Let yourself think big and open up your true potential.

Your life is not there for you to just plod along and live in routine that doesn't serve you or fill you with complete joy and accomplishment.

This future plan is a way of lighting up your soul and making you realise that anxiety is NOT your future. YOU are!

Come on lovely – dream and aim high, I'm rooting for you!

Here is mine;

In 5 years' time I will be;

> A best-selling author worldwide and have sold over 1 million copies of this book, as well as over 1 million copies of my second book (you will find out about that soon enough!)
>
> Living with my family in a beautiful home by the sea and waves, with a balcony outside my bedroom, that I can open the doors to every morning and stand and enjoy the view. The country is yet to be decided, but sunshine and warmth will feature heavily at my dream home!
>
> I will be speaking worldwide about anxiety and mental health, empowering women left, right and centre – I will be the name and face of overcoming anxiety, giving women all over the globe the joy they have been missing.
>
> I will be truly happy with my family, my close friends and the routines I live by daily. Which will include morning yoga or meditation, weekly massages and walks along the beach and a blow dry once a month.

I could go on and on, but the key is;

- Be specific
- Paint a picture of your future life in your mind
- Bring emotion into the equation to strengthen the image
- Make it personal to you
- Don't limit your dreams, ideas and plans

Once you have this plan, you know what you are working towards and you know what you are building upon in the here and now.

'Anxiety is NOT your future. YOU are'

WOW!

Here we are. The book may have reached its final pages, but our journey together is far from over.

Your happiness, relationships and mind-set are your priority now.

Some key things I want you to remember when anxiety tries to show up or a little blip happens;

- Don't beat yourself up, you are only human.

The more you persevere and have patience with yourself, the easier it will become to bounce back and manage the anxiety.

- Ask yourself questions.

I cannot stress this enough. Do not ignore the emotion. Take notice of it and start unpicking it. Awareness and understanding are vital in this process.

Why do you feel that way? What triggered it? Where are you? Can you do anything to change it?

- Have a pity party.

Give yourself time. TIME! Just spend 5 minutes feeling the feeling. Don't rush anything, force anything or change anything. Just spend a moment allowing the emotion to be there and listen to how it is making you feel. Once you know how you DON'T want to feel, it will be so much easier for you to correct it and move on.

- You are NOT crazy.

I am here with you every step of the way. I have been where you are and I have felt how you feel. You are not alone and you are not crazy. You are learning and you are taking action. Be proud of that!

- Focus on progress, not perfection.

Don't focus on the one time something doesn't work out, focus on all the times you do something that would have been a struggle before. All the times you put yourself into a new situation and grow. Reward yourself for every small step and every slice of progress because these lead to the bigger changes and transformations.

- Do things you enjoy doing.

Don't say yes to everything and 'people please'. Remember your love list. Use it and apply it to your life and routines as often as you possibly can.

Last but not least;

I am so very proud of you and I am so grateful that we have spent this time together and you have allowed me into your life.

Keep being amazing and don't stop working towards your happiness – you deserve the very best my lovely, you really do.

If you haven't already, here are some action points for you;

- Review this book on Amazon

My goal is to support and empower over 1 million wonderful women worldwide (all the W's) and that can only happen if the word continues to spread, which is where you come in! Review away and make my dreams come true ☺

- Join my Facebook group and business page

www.facebook.com/AHappyMind1

- Follow my Instagram and see all behind the scenes

www.instagram.com/a.happy.mind

- Book your discovery call with me, if you are ready for 1:1 coaching and to dig deeper

www.ahappymind.co.uk

Let's Kick Anxiety's Butt!

- Make sure you complete the selfie challenge and send me your pictures, tag me and share the love on all the places I have listed above. I want to see your lovely face!

Once again, thank you for allowing me to be part this journey with you, I am so excited to see the changes and amazing things you will be creating in your future.

All my love,

Sam x.x.x

Let's Kick Anxiety's Butt!

Let's Kick Anxiety's Butt!

Printed in Great Britain
by Amazon